Cambridge Plain Texts

DONNE

SERMONS

XV AND LXVI

T0346131

DONNE

SERMONS

XV and LXVI

CAMBRIDGE
AT THE UNIVERSITY PRESS
1921

CAMBRIDGE UNIVERSITY PRESS
Cambridge, New York, Melbourne, Madrid, Cape Town,
Singapore, São Paulo, Delhi, Mexico City

Cambridge University Press
The Edinburgh Building, Cambridge CB2 8RU, UK

Published in the United States of America by Cambridge University Press, New York

www.cambridge.org
Information on this title: www.cambridge.org/9781107638174

© Cambridge University Press 1921

First published 1921
Re-issued 2013

A catalogue record for this publication is available from the British Library

ISBN 978-1-107-63817-4 Paperback

NOTE

EVERY student of our literature knows the poems of John Donne (1573–1631); early compositions, slight in bulk, but portentous and amazing as everything he wrote, from first to last, was portentous and amazing. They mark an epoch in that undying form of art, the lyric; they laid their spell over two generations of verse-makers; their music, constantly broken by passion or by equally fierce contempt of passion, still haunts and disturbs. But few consider his Sermons, in which lie embedded ingots of the most splendid prose ever fused and moulded by English brain and tongue working together. The vogue of the Sermon has passed. One might almost say that the honour of the living voice, whether in speech or in song, has passed. But there was a Golden Age of the Pulpit in England: and of that age, in that pulpit, with Lancelot Andrewes, Ussher, Hall and the later-born Jeremy Taylor for nearest rivals, the great Dean of St Paul's stands as the most tremendous figure. His learning was great even among men of that most learned age; his voice marvellous; his presence awful. He seldom or never preached for less than an hour, often much longer, but (*teste* Walton) would hold his vast audience shaken and trembling; and was always most impressive when he wrestled with the theme of Death. For his mind—ever mystical, yet imperfectly, because full of animal heat and indignant and restlessly curious—ever played on close terms with our last enemy. He surrendered himself savagely to face its most dreadful aspects, corruption and the worm. He sat for his portrait in his shroud and slept with the picture by his bedside. More fancifully than St Paul, yet in solemn act, he died daily.

Here are two of his grandest Sermons on that theme, with their assurance of Death swallowed up in Victory.

Q.

December 1920.

SERMON XV

Preached at White-hall, March 8, 1621.

1 COR. 15. 26. *The last Enemie that shall be destroyed, is Death.*

THIS is a Text of the Resurrection, and it is not Easter yet; but it is Easter Eve; All Lent, is but the Vigill, the Eve of Easter: to so long a Festivall as never shall end, the Resurrection, wee may well begin the Eve betimes. Forty yeares long was God grieved for that Generation which he loved; let us be content to humble our selves forty daies, to be fitter for that glory which we expect. In the Booke of God there are many *Songs*; there is but one *Lamentation*: And that one Song of *Solomon*, nay some one of *Davids* hundred and fiftie Psalmes, is longer then the whole booke of Lamentations. Make way to an everlasting Easter by a short Lent, to an undeterminable glory, by a temporary humiliation. You must weepe these teares, teares of contrition, teares of mortification, before God will wipe all teares from your eyes; You must dye this death, this death of the righteous, the death to sin, before this *last enemy*, *Death*, shalbe destroyed in you, and you made partakers of everlasting life in soule and body too.

Our division shall be but a short, and our whole exercise but a larger paraphrase upon the words. The words imply first, That the Kingdome of Christ, which must be perfected, must be accomplished, (because all things must be subdued unto him) is not yet perfected, not accomplished yet. Why? what lacks it? It lacks the bodies of Men, which yet lie under the dominion of another. When we shall also see by that Metaphor which the Holy Ghost chooseth to expresse that in, which is that there is *Hostis*, and so *Militia*, an enemie, and a warre, and therefore that Kingdome is not perfected, that he places perfect happinesse, and perfect glory, in perfect peace. But then how far is any State consisting of many men, how far the state, and condition of any one man in particular, from this perfect peace? How truly a warfare is this life, if the Kingdome of Heaven it selfe, have not this peace in perfection? And it hath it not, *Quia hostis*, because there is an enemy: though that enemy shall not overthrow it, yet because it plots, and workes, and machinates, and would overthrow it, this is a defect in that peace.

Who then is this enemy? An enemy that may thus far thinke himselfe equall to God, that as no man ever saw God, and lived; so no man ever saw this enemy and lived, for it is Death; And in this may thinke himselfe in number superiour to God, that many men live who shall never see God; But *Quis homo*, is *Davids* question, which was never answered, *Is there any man that lives, and shall not see death?* An enemie that is so well victualled against man, as that he cannot want as long as there are men, for he feeds upon man himselfe. And so well armed against Man, as that he cannot want Munition, while there are men, for he fights with our weapons, our owne faculties, nay our calamities, yea our owne pleasures are our death. And therefore he is *Novissimus hostis*, saith the Text, *The last enemy*.

We have other Enemies; Satan about us, sin within us; but the power of both those, this enemie shall destroy; but when they are destroyed, he shall retaine a hostile, and triumphant dominion over us. But *Vsque quo Domine?* How long O Lord? for ever? No, *Abolebitur:* wee see this Enemy all the way, and all the way we feele him; but we shall see him destroyed; *Abolebitur.* But how? or when? At, and by the resurrection of our bodies: for as upon my expiration, my transmigration from hence, as soone as my soule enters into Heaven, I shall be able to say to the Angels, I am of the same stuffe as you, spirit, and spirit, and therefore let me stand with you, and looke upon the face of your God, and my God; so at the Resurrection of this body, I shall be able to say to the Angel of the great Councell, the Son of God, Christ Jesus himselfe, I am of the same stuffe as you, Body and body, Flesh and flesh, and therefore let me sit downe with you, at the right hand of the Father in an everlasting security from this last enemie, who is now destroyed, death. And in these seven steps we shall passe apace, and yet cleerely through this paraphrase.

We begin with this; That the Kingdome of Heaven hath not all that it must have to a consummate perfection, till it have bodies too. In those infinite millions of millions of generations, in which the holy, blessed, and glorious Trinity enjoyed themselves one another, and no more, they thought not their glory so perfect, but that it might receive an addition from creatures; and therefore they made a world, a materiall world, a corporeall world, they would have bodies. In that noble part of that world which *Moses* cals the Firmament, that great expansion from Gods chaire to his footstoole, from Heaven to earth, there was a defect, which God did not supply that day, nor the next, but the fourth day, he did; for that day he made those bodies, those great, and lightsome bodies, the Sunne, and Moone, and Starres, and placed them in the Firmament. So also the Heaven of Heavens, the Presence Chamber of God himselfe, expects the presence of our bodies.

No State upon earth, can subsist without those bodies, Men of their owne. For men that are supplied from others, may either in necessity, or in indignation, be withdrawne, and so that State which stood upon forraine legs, sinks. Let the head be gold, and the armes silver, and the belly brasse, if the feete be clay, Men that may slip, and molder away, all is but an Image, all is but a dreame of an Image: for forraine helps are rather crutches then legs. There must be bodies, Men, and able bodies, able men; Men that eate the good things of the land, their owne figges and olives; Men not macerated with extortions: They are glorified bodies that make up the kingdome of Heaven; bodies that partake of the good of the State, that make up the State. Bodies, able bodies, and lastly, bodies inanimated with one soule: one vegetative soule, all must be sensible and compassionate of one anothers miserie; and especially the Immortall soule, one supreame soule, one Religion. For as God hath made us under good Princes, a great example of all that, Abundance of Men, Men that live like men, men united in one Religion, so wee need not goe farre for an example of a slippery, and uncertaine being, where they must stand upon others Mens men, and must over-load all men with exactions, and distortions, and convulsions, and earthquakes in the multiplicity of Religions.

The Kingdome of Heaven must have bodies; Kingdomes of the earth must have them; and if upon the earth thou beest in the way to Heaven, thou must have a body too, a body of thine owne, a body in thy possession: for thy body hath thee, and not thou it, if thy body tyrannize over thee. If thou canst not withdraw thine eye from an object of tentation, or withhold thy hand from subscribing against thy conscience, nor turne thine eare from a popular, and seditious Libell, what hast thou towards a man? Thou hast no soule, nay thou hast no body: There is a body, but thou hast it not, it is not thine, it is not in thy power. Thy body will rebell against thee even in a sin: It will not performe a sin, when, and where thou wouldst have it. Much more will it rebell against any good worke, till thou have imprinted *Stigmata Iesu, The Markes of the Lord Iesus*, which were but exemplar in him, but are essentiall, and necessary to thee, abstinencies, and such discreete disciplines, and mortifications, as may subdue that body to thee, and make it thine: for till then it is but thine enemy, and maintaines a warre against thee; and war, and enemie is the Metaphore which the holy Ghost hath taken here to expresse a want, a kind of imperfectnesse even in Heaven it selfe. *Bellum Symbolum mali.* As peace is of all goodnesse, so warre is an embleme, a Hieroglyphique, of all misery; And that is our second step in this paraphrase.

If the feete of them that preach peace, be beautifull, (And, *O how beautifull are the feete of them that preach peace?* The Prophet *Isaiah* askes the question, 52. 7.

And the Prophet *Nahum* askes it, 1. 15. and the Apostle
S. *Paul* askes it, *Rom.* 10. 15. They all aske it, but none
answers it) who shall answer us, if we aske, How
beautifull is his face, who is the Author of this peace,
when we shall see that in the glory of Heaven, the
Center of all true peace? It was the inheritance of
Christ Jesus upon the earth, he had it at his birth,
he brought it with him, *Glory be to God on high,
peace upon earth.* It was his purchase upon earth,
He made peace (indeed he bought peace) *through the
blood of his Crosse.* It was his Testament, when he
went from earth; *Peace I leave with you, my peace
I give unto you.* Divide with him in that blessed
Inheritance, partake with him in that blessed Pur-
chase, enrich thy selfe with that blessed Legacy, his
Peace.

Let the whole world be in thy consideration as one
house; and then consider in that, in the peacefull
harmony of creatures, in the peacefull succession, and
connexion of causes, and effects, the peace of Nature.
Let this Kingdome, where God hath blessed thee with
a being, be the Gallery, the best roome of that house,
and consider in the two walls of that Gallery, the
Church and the State, the peace of a royall, and a
religious Wisedome; Let thine owne family be a
Cabinet in this Gallery, and finde in all the boxes
thereof, in the severall duties of Wife, and Children,
and servants, the peace of vertue, and of the father
and mother of all vertues, active discretion, passive
obedience; and then lastly, let thine owne bosome be
the secret box, and reserve in this Cabinet, and then
the best Jewell in the best Cabinet, and that in the
best Gallery of the best house that can be had, peace

with the Creature, peace in the Church, peace in the
State, peace in thy house, peace in thy heart, is a faire
Modell, and a lovely designe even of the heavenly
Jerusalem which is *Visio pacis*, where there is no object
but peace.

And therefore the holy Ghost to intimate to us, that
happy perfectnesse, which wee shall have at last, and
not till then, chooses the Metaphor of an enemy, and
enmity, to avert us from looking for true peace from
any thing that presents it selfe in the way. Neither
truly could the holy Ghost imprint more horror by
any word, then that which intimates war, as the word
enemy does. It is but a little way that the Poet hath
got in description of war, *Iam seges est*, that now, that
place is ploughed where the great City stood: for it
is not so great a depopulation to translate a City from
Merchants to husbandmen, from shops to ploughes,
as it is from many Husbandmen to one Shepheard,
and yet that hath beene often done. And all that, at
most, is but a depopulation, it is not a devastation,
that Troy was ploughed. But, when the Prophet
Isaiah comes to the devastation, to the extermination
of a war, he expresses it first thus; *Where there were a
thousand Vineyards at a cheape rate, all the land become
briars and thornes:* That is much; but there is more,
*The earth shall be removed out of her place; that Land,
that Nation, shall no more be called that Nation, nor
that Land:* But, yet more then that too; Not onely,
not that people, but no other shall ever inhabit it. *It
shall never be inhabited from generation to generation,
neither shall Shepheard be there; Not onely no Mer-
chant, nor Husbandman, but no depopulator: none but
Owles, and Ostriches, and Satyres,* Indeed God knowes

what, *Ochim*, and *Ziim*, words which truly we cannot translate.

In a word, the horror of War is best discerned in the company he keeps, in his associates. And when the Prophet *Gad* brought *War* into the presence of *David*, there came with him *Famine*, and *Pestilence*. And when Famine entred, we see the effects; It brought Mothers to eat their Children of a span long; that is, as some Expositors take it, to take medicines to procure abortions, to cast their Children, that they might have Children to eate. And when War's other companion, the Pestilence entred, we see the effects of that too: In lesse then half the time that it was threatned for, it devoured threescore and ten thousand of *Davids* men; and yet for all the vehemence, the violence, the impetuousnesse of this Pestilence, *David* chose this Pestilence rather then a War. *Militia* and *Malitia*, are words of so neare a sound, as that the vulgat Edition takes them as one. For where the Prophet speaking of the miseries that Hierusalem had suffered, sayes, *Finita militia ejus.* Let her *warfare* be at an end, they reade, *Finita malitia ejus*, Let her *misery* be at an end; War and Misery is all one thing. But is there any of this in heaven? Even the Saints in heaven lack something of the consummation of their happinesse, *Quia hostis*, because they have an enemy. And that is our third and next step.

Michael and his Angels fought against the devill and his Angels; though that war ended in victory, yet (taking that war, as divers Expositors doe, for the fall of Angels) that Kingdome lost so many inhabitants, as that all the soules of all that shall be saved, shall

but fill up the places of them that fell, and so make
that Kingdome but as well as it was before that war:
So ill effects accompany even the most victorious war.
There is no war in heaven, yet all is not well, because
there is an enemy; for that enemy would kindle a war
again, but that he remembers how ill he sped last time
he did so. It is not an enemy that invades neither, but
only detaines: he detaines the bodies of the Saints
which are in heaven, and therefore is an enemy to
the Kingdome of Christ; He that detaines the soules
of men in Superstition, he that detaines the hearts
and allegeance of Subjects in an hæsitation, a vacilla-
tion, an irresolution, where they shall fix them,
whether upon their Soveraign, or a forraigne power,
he is in the notion, and acceptation of enemy in this
Text; an enemy, though no hostile act be done. It is
not a war, it is but an enemy; not an invading, but a
detaining enemy; and then this enemy is but one
enemy, and yet he troubles, and retards the consummation of that Kingdome.

Antichrist alone is enemy enough; but never carry
this consideration beyond thy self. As long as there
remaines in thee one sin, or the sinfull gain of that
one sin, so long there is one enemy, and where there
is one enemy, there is no peace. Gardners that husband their ground to the best advantage, sow all their
seeds in such order, one under another, that their
Garden is alwayes full of that which is then in season.
If thou sin with that providence, with that seasonable-
nesse, that all thy spring, thy youth be spent in wantonnesse, all thy Summer, thy middle-age in ambition,
and the wayes of preferment, and thy Autumne, thy
Winter in indevotion and covetousnesse, though thou

have no farther taste of licentiousnesse, in thy middle-
age, thou hast thy satiety in that sin, nor of ambition
in thy last yeares, thou hast accumulated titles of
honour, yet all the way thou hast had one enemy, and
therefore never any perfect peace. But who is this
one enemy in this Text? As long as we put it off, and
as loath as we are to look this enemy in the face, yet
we must, though it be Death. And this is *Vestigium
quartum*, The fourth and next step in this paraphrase.

Surge & descende in domum figuli, says the Prophet
Ieremy, that is, say the Expositors, to the consideration of thy Mortality. It is *Surge, descende, Arise and
go down:* A descent with an ascension: Our grave is
upward, and our heart is upon *Iacobs* Ladder, in the
way, and nearer to heaven. Our daily Funerals are
some Emblemes of that; for though we be laid down
in the earth after, yet we are lifted up upon mens
shoulders before. We rise in the descent to death,
and so we do in the descent to the contemplation of
it. In all the Potters house, is there one vessell made
of better stuffe then clay? There is his matter. And
of all formes, a Circle is the perfectest, and art thou
loath to make up that Circle, with returning to the
earth again?

Thou must, though thou be loath. *Fortasse*, sayes
S. *Augustine*, That word of contingency, of casualty,
Perchance, *In omnibus ferme rebus, præterquam in morte
locum habet:* It hath roome in all humane actions ex-
cepting death. He makes his example thus: such a
man is married; where he would, or at least where he
must, where his parents, or his Gardian will have him;
shall he have Children? *Fortasse*, sayes he, They are
a yong couple, perchance they shall: And shall those

Children be sons? *Fortasse*, they are of a strong con-
stitution, perchance they shall: And shall those sons
live to be men? *Fortasse*, they are from healthy parents,
perchance they shall: And when they have lived to be
men, shall they be good men? Such as good men may
be glad they may live? *Fortasse*, still; They are of
vertuous parents, it may be they shall: But when they
are come to that *Morientur*, shall those good men die?
here, sayes that Father, the *Fortasse* vanishes; here it
is *omnino*, *certè*, *sine dubitatione*; infallibly, inevitably,
irrecoverably they must die. Doth not man die even
in his birth? The breaking of prison is death, and
what is our birth, but a breaking of prison? As soon
as we were clothed by God, our very apparell was an
Embleme of death. In the skins of dead beasts, he
covered the skins of dying men. Assoon as God set
us on work, our very occupation was an Embleme of
death; It was to digge the earth; not to digge pitfals
for other men, but graves for our selves. Hath any
man here forgot to day, that yesterday is dead? And
the Bell tolls for to day, and will ring out anon; and
for as much of every one of us, as appertaines to this
day. *Quotidiè morimur, & tamen nos esse æternos
putamus*, sayes S. *Hierome*; We die every day, and we
die all the day long; and because we are not absolutely
dead, we call that an eternity, an eternity of dying:
And is there comfort in that state? why, that is the
state of hell it self, Eternall dying, and not dead.

But for this there is enough said, by the Morall
man; (that we may respite divine proofes, for divine
points anon, for our severall Resurrections) for this
death is meerly naturall, and it is enough that the
morall man sayes, *Mors lex, tributum, officium mor-*

talium. First it is *lex*, you were born under that law, upon that condition to die: so it is a rebellious thing not to be content to die, it opposes the Law. Then it is *Tributum*, an imposition which nature the Queen of this world layes upon us, and which she will take, when and where she list; here a yong man, there an old man, here a happy, there a miserable man; And so it is a seditious thing not to be content to die, it opposes the prerogative. And lastly, it is *Officium*, men are to have their turnes, to take their time, and then to give way by death to successors; and so it is *Incivile, inofficiosum*, not to be content to die, it opposes the frame and form of government. It comes equally to us all, and makes us all equall when it comes. The ashes of an Oak in the Chimney, are no Epitaph of that Oak, to tell me how high or how large that was; It tels me not what flocks it sheltered while it stood, nor what men it hurt when it fell. The dust of great persons graves is speechlesse too, it sayes nothing, it distinguishes nothing: As soon the dust of a wretch whom thou wouldest not, as of a Prince whom thou couldest not look upon, will trouble thine eyes, if the winde blow it thither; and when a whirle-winde hath blowne the dust of the Church-yard into the Church, and the man sweeps out the dust of the Church into the Church-yard, who will undertake to sift those dusts again, and to pronounce, This is the Patrician, this is the noble flowre, and this the yeomanly, this the Plebeian bran. So is the death of *Iesabel* (*Iesabel* was a Queen) expressed; *They shall not say, this is Iesabel*; not only not wonder that it is, nor pity that it should be, but they shall not say, they shall not know, This is *Iesabel*. It comes to all, to all alike; but

not alike welcome to all. To die too willingly, out of
impatience to wish, or out of violence to hasten death,
or to die too unwillingly, to murmure at Gods purpose
revealed by age, or by sicknesse, are equall distempers;
and to harbour a disobedient loathnesse all the way,
or to entertain it at last, argues but an irreligious
ignorance; An ignorance, that death is in nature but
Expiratio, a breathing out, and we do that every minute;
An ignorance that God himself took a day to rest in,
and a good mans grave is his Sabbath; An ignorance
that *Abel* the best of those whom we can compare
with him, was the first that dyed. Howsoever, when-
soever, all times are Gods times: *Vocantur boni ne
diutiùs vexentur à noxiis, mali ne diutiùs bonos perse-
quantur*, God cals the good to take them from their
dangers, and God takes the bad to take them from
their triumph. And therefore neither grudge that thou
goest, nor that worse stay, for God can make his profit
of both; *Aut ideo vivit ut corrigatur, aut ideo ut per
illum bonus exerceatur*; God reprieves him to mend
him, or to make another better by his exercise; and
not to exult in the misery of another, but to glorifie
God in the wayes of his justice, let him know, *Quan-
tumcunque serò, subitò ex hac vita tollitur, qui finem præ-
videre nescivit:* How long soever he live, how long soever he lie sick, that man dies a sudden death, who
never thought of it. If we consider death in S. *Pauls
Statutum est, It is decreed that all men must die*, there
death is indifferent; If we consider it in his *Mori
lucrum, that it is an advantage to die*, there death is
good; and so much the vulgat Edition seemes to
intimate, when (*Deut.* 30. 19.) whereas we reade, I
have set before you life and death, that reades it,

Vitam & bonum, Life, and that which is good. If
then death be at the worst indifferent, and to the good,
good, how is it *Hostis*, an enemy to the Kingdome of
Christ? for that also is *Vestigium quintum*, the fift and
next step in this paraphrase.

First God did not make death, saies the Wiseman,
And therefore S. *Augustine* makes a reasonable prayer
to God, *Ne permittas Domine quod non fecisti, dominari
Creaturæ quam fecisti*; Suffer not O Lord, death,
whom thou didst not make, to have dominion over
me whom thou didst. Whence then came death? The
same Wiseman hath shewed us the father, Through
envy of the devill, came death into the world; and a
wiser then he, the holy Ghost himselfe hath shewed
us the Mother, *By sin came death into the world*. But
yet if God have naturalized death, taken death into
the number of his servants, and made Death his Com-
missioner to punish sin, and he doe but that, how is
Death an enemy? First, he was an enemy in invading
Christ, who was not in his Commission, because he
had no sin; and still he is an enemie, because still he
adheres to the enemy. Death hangs upon the edge of
every persecutors sword; and upon the sting of every
calumniators, and accusers tongue. In the Bull of
Phalaris, in the Bulls of Basan, in the Buls of Babylon,
the shrewdest Buls of all, in temporall, in spirituall
persecutions, ever since God put an enmity between
Man, and the Serpent, from the time of *Cain* who
began in a murther, to the time of Antichrist, who
proceeds in Massacres, Death hath adhered to the
enemy, and so is an enemy.

Death hath a Commission, *Stipendium peccati mors
est, The reward of sin is Death*, but where God gives

a Supersedeas, upon that Commission, *Vivo Ego, nolo mortem, As I live saith the Lord, I would have no sinner dye*, not dye the second death, yet Death proceeds to that execution: And whereas the enemy, whom he adheres to, the Serpent himselfe, hath power but *In calcaneo*, upon the heele, the lower, the mortall part, the body of man, *Death is come up into our windowes*, saith the Prophet, into our best lights, our understandings, and benights us there, either with ignorance, before sin, or with senselesnesse after: And a Sheriffe that should burne him, who were condemned to be hanged, were a murderer, though that man must have dyed: To come in by the doore, by the way of sicknesse upon the body, is, but to come in at the window by the way of sin, is not deaths Commission; God opens not that window.

So then he is an enemy, for they that adhere to the enemy are enemies: And adhering is not only a present subministration of supply to the enemy (for that death doth not) but it is also a disposition to assist the enemy, then when he shall be strong enough to make benefit of that assistance. And so death adheres; when sin and Satan have weakned body and minde, death enters upon both. And in that respect he is *Vltimus hostis*, the last enemy, and that is *Sextum vestigium*, our sixth and next step in this paraphrase.

Death is the last, and in that respect the worst enemy. In an enemy, that appeares at first, when we are or may be provided against him, there is some of that, which we call Honour: but in the enemie that reserves himselfe unto the last, and attends our weake estate, there is more danger. Keepe it, where I intend it, in that which is my spheare, the Conscience: If mine enemie meet me betimes in my youth, in an object of tentation, (so *Iosephs* enemie met him in *Putifars* Wife) yet if I doe not adhere to this enemy, dwell upon a delightfull meditation of that sin, if I doe not fuell, and foment that sin, assist and encourage that sin, by high diet, wanton discourse, other provocation, I shall have reason on my side, and I shall have grace on my side, and I shall have the History of a thousand that have perished by that sin, on my side; Even Spittles will give me souldiers to fight for me, by their miserable example against that sin; nay perchance sometimes the vertue of that woman, whom I sollicite, will assist me. But when I lye under the hands of that enemie, that hath reserved himselfe to the last, to my last bed, then when I shall be able to stir no limbe in any other measure then a Feaver or a Palsie shall shake them, when everlasting darknesse shall have an inchoation in the present dimnesse of mine eyes, and the everlasting gnashing in the present chattering of my teeth, and the everlasting worme in the present gnawing of the Agonies of my body, and anguishes of my minde, when the last enemie shall watch my remedilesse body, and my disconsolate soule there, there, where not the Physitian, in his way, perchance not the Priest in his, shall be able to give any assistance, And when he hath sported himselfe with my misery upon that stage, my death-bed, shall shift the Scene, and throw me from that bed, into the grave, and there triumph over me, God knowes, how many generations, till the Redeemer, my Redeemer, the Redeemer of all me, body, as well as soule, come againe; As death is *Novissimus hostis*, the enemy which watches me, at my last weaknesse, and shall hold me, when I

shall be no more, till that Angel come, *Who shall say,
and sweare that time shall be no more*, in that consideration, in that apprehension, he is the powerfullest, the
fearefulest enemy; and yet even there this enemy *Abolebitur*, he shall be destroyed, which is, *Septimum vestigium*, our seventh and last step in this paraphrase.

This destruction, this abolition of this last enemy,
is by the Resurrection; for the Text is part of an
argument for the Resurrection. And truly, it is a
faire intimation, and testimony of an everlasting end
in that state of the Resurrection (that no time shall end
it) that we have it presented to us in all the parts of
time; in the past, in the present, and in the future.
We had a Resurrection in prophecy; we have a Resurrection in the present working of Gods Spirit; we
shall have a Resurrection in the finall consummation.
The Prophet speaks in the future, *He will swallow up
death in victory*, there it is *Abolebit:* All the Euange-
lists speak historically, of matter of fact, in them it is
Abolevit. And here in this Apostle, it is in the present,
Aboletur, now he is destroyed. And this exhibites unto
us a threefold occasion of advancing our devotion, in
considering a threefold Resurrection; First, a Resurrection from dejections and calamities in this world,
a Temporary Resurrection; Secondly, a Resurrection
from sin, a Spirituall Resurrection; and then a Resurrection from the grave, a finall Resurrection.

A calamitate; When the Prophets speak of a Resurrection in the old Testament, for the most part their
principall intention is, upon a temporall restitution
from calamities that oppresse them then. Neither
doth *Calvin* carry those emphaticall words, which are
so often cited for a proofe of the last Resurrection:

That he knows his Redeemer lives, that he knows he shall
stand the last man upon earth, that though his body be
destroyed, yet in his flesh and with his eyes he shall see
God, to any higher sense then so, that how low soever
he bee brought, to what desperate state soever he be
reduced in the eyes of the world, yet he assures himself of a Resurrection, a reparation, a restitution to his
former bodily health, and worldly fortune which he
had before. And such a Resurrection we all know
Iob had.

In that famous, and most considerable propheticall
vision which God exhibited to *Ezekiel*, where God set
the Prophet in a valley of very many, and very dry
bones, and invites the severall joynts to knit again,
tyes them with their old sinews, and ligaments, clothes
them in their old flesh, wraps them in their old skin,
and cals life into them again, Gods principall intention
in that vision was thereby to give them an assurance
of a Resurrection from their present calamity, not but
that there is also good evidence of the last Resurrection
in that vision too; Thus far God argues with them *à*
re nota; from that which they knew before, the finall
Resurrection, he assures them that which they knew
not till then, a present Resurrection from those pressures: Remember by this vision that which you all
know already, that at last I shall re-unite the dead,
and dry bones of all men in a generall Resurrection:
And then if you remember, if you consider, if you
look upon that, can you doubt, but that I who can do
that, can also recollect you, from your present desperation, and give you a Resurrection to your former temporall happinesse? And this truly arises pregnantly,
necessarily out of the Prophets answer; God asks him

there, *Son of man, can these bones live?* And he answers, *Domine tu nôsti, O Lord God thou knowest.* The Prophet answers according to Gods intention in the question. If that had been for their living in the last Resurrection, *Ezekiel* would have answered God as *Martha* answered Christ, when he said, *Thy brother Lazarus shall rise again, I know that he shall rise again at the Resurrection at the last day*; but when the question was, whether men so macerated, so scattered in this world, could have a Resurrection to their former temporall happinesse here, that puts the Prophet to his *Domine tu nôsti*, It is in thy breast to propose it, it is in thy hand to execute it, whether thou do it, or do it not, thy name be glorified; It fals not within our conjecture, which way it shall please thee to take for this Resurrection, *Domine tu nôsti*, Thou Lord, and thou only knowest; Which is also the sense of those words, *Others were tortured, and accepted not a deliverance, that they might obtain a better Resurrection:* A present deliverance had been a Resurrection, but to be the more sure of a better hereafter, they lesse respected that; According to that of our Saviour, *He that findes his life, shall lose it*; He that fixeth himself too earnestly upon this Resurrection, shall lose a better.

This is then the propheticall Resurrection for the future, but a future in this world; That if Rulers take counsell against the Lord, the Lord shall have their counsell in derision; If they take armes against the Lord, the Lord shall break their Bows, and cut their Speares in sunder; If they hisse, and gnash their teeth, and say, we have swallowed him up; If we be made their by-word, their parable, their proverb, their libell, the theame and burden of their songs, as *Iob* complaines, yet whatsoever fall upon me, damage, distresse, scorn, or *Hostis ultimus*, death it self, that death which we consider here, death of possessions, death of estimation, death of health, death of contentment, yet *Abolebitur*, it shall be destroyed in a Resurrection, in the return of the light of Gods countenance upon me even in this world. And this is the first Resurrection.

But this first Resurrection, which is but from temporall calamities, doth so little concerne a true and established Christian, whether it come or no, (for still *Iobs* Basis is his Basis, and his Centre, *Etiamsi occiderit*, though he kill me, kill me, kill me, in all these severall deaths, and give me no Resurrection in this world, yet I will trust in him) as that, as though this first resurrection were no resurrection, not to be numbred among the resurrections, S. *Iohn* calls that which we call the second, which is from sin, the first resurrection: *Blessed and holy is he, who hath part in the first resurrection:* And this resurrection, Christ implies, when he saies, *Verely, verely, I say unto you, the houre is comming, and now is, when the dead shall heare the voyce of the Son of God; and they that heare it shall live:* That is, by the voyce of the word of life, the Gospell of repentance, they shall have a spirituall resurrection to a new life.

S. *Austine* and *Lactantius* both were so hard in beleeving the roundnesse of the earth, that they thought that those *homines pensiles*, as they call them, those men that hang upon the other cheek of the face of the earth, those Antipodes, whose feet are directly against ours, must necessarily fall from the earth, if the earth be round. But whither should they fall? If they fall, they must fall upwards, for heaven is above them too, as it is to us. So if the spirituall Antipodes of this world, the Sons of God, that walk with feet opposed in wayes contrary to the sons of men, shall be said to fall, when they fall to repentance, to mortification, to a religious negligence, and contempt of the pleasures of this life, truly their fall is upwards, they fall towards heaven. *God gives breath unto the people upon the earth*, sayes the Prophet, *Et spiritum his, qui calcant illam.* Our Translation carries that no farther, but that *God gives breath to people upon the earth, and spirit to them that walk thereon*; But *Irenæus* makes a usefull difference between *afflatus* and *spiritus*, that God gives breath to all upon earth, but his spirit onely to them, who tread in a religious scorne upon earthly things.

Is it not a strange phrase of the Apostle, *Mortifie your members; fornication, uncleanenesse, inordinate affections?* He does not say, mortifie your members against those sins, but he calls those very sins, the members of our bodies, as though we were elemented and compacted of nothing but sin, till we come to this resurrection, this mortification, which is indeed our vivification; *Till we beare in our body, the dying of our Lord Iesus, that the life also of Iesus may be made manifest in our body.* God may give the other resurrection from worldly misery, and not give this. A widow may be rescued from the sorrow and solitarinesse of that state, by having a plentifull fortune; there she hath one resurrection; but *the widow that liveth in pleasure, is dead while she lives*; shee hath no second resurrection; and so in that sense, even this Chappell may be a Church-yard, men may stand, and sit, and kneele, and yet be dead; and any Chamber alone may be a *Golgotha*, a place of dead mens bones, of men not come to this resurrection, which is the renunciation of their beloved sin.

It was inhumanely said by *Vitellius*, upon the death of *Otho*, when he walked in the field of carcasses, where the battle was fought; O how sweet a perfume is a dead enemy! But it is a divine saying to thy soule, O what a savor of life, unto life, is the death of a beloved sin! What an Angelicall comfort was that to *Ioseph* and *Mary* in Ægypt, after the death of *Herod*, *Arise, for they are dead, that sought the childes life!* And even that comfort is multiplied upon thy soul, when the Spirit of God saies to thee, Arise, come to this resurrection: for that *Herod*, that sin, that sought the life, the everlasting life of this childe, the childe of God, thy soule, is dead, dead by repentance, dead by mortification. The highest cruelty that story relates, or Poets imagine, is when a persecutor will not afford a miserable man death, not be so mercifull to him, as to take his life. Thou hast made thy sin, thy soule, thy life; inanimated all thy actions, all thy purposes with that sin. *Miserere animæ tuæ*, be so mercifull to thy selfe, as to take away that life by mortification, by repentance, and thou art come to this Resurrection: and though a man may have the former resurrection, and not this, peace in his fortune, and yet not peace in his conscience, yet whosoever hath this second, hath an infallible seale of the third resurrection too, to a fulnesse of glory in body, as well as in soule. For *Spiritus maturam efficit carnem, & capacem incorruptelæ*; this resurrection by the spirit, mellowes the body of man, and makes that capable of everlasting glory, which is the last weapon, by which the last enemy death, shall be destroyed; *A morte*.

Upon that pious ground that all Scriptures were written for us, as we are Christians, that all Scriptures conduce to the proofe of Christ, and of the Christian State, it is the ordinary manner of the Fathers to make all that *David* speaks historically of himselfe, and all that the Prophet speaks futurely of the Jews, if those places may be referred to Christ, to referre them to Christ primarily, and but by reflection, and in a second consideration upon *David*, or upon the Jews. Thereupon doe the Fathers (truly I think more generally more unanimely then in any other place of Scripture) take that place of *Ezekiel* which we spake of before, to be primarily intended of the last resurrection, & but secundarily of the Jews restitution. But *Gasper Sanctius* a learned Jesuit, (that is not so rare, but an ingenuous Jesuit too) though he be bound by the Councel of Trent, to interpret Scriptures according to the Fathers, yet here he acknowledges the whole truth, that Gods purpose was to prove, by that which they did know, which was the generall resurrection, that which they knew not, their temporall restitution. *Tertullian* is vehement at first, but after, more supple. *Allegoricæ Scripturæ*, saies he, *resurrectionem subradiant aliæ, aliæ determinant:* Some figurative places of Scripture doe intimate a resurrection, and some manifest it; and of those manifest places he takes this vision of *Ezekiel* to be one. But he comes after to this, *Sit & corporum, & rerum, & meâ nihil interest*; let it signifie a temporall resurrection, so it may signifie the generall resurrection of our bodies too, saies he, and I am well satisfied; and then the truth satisfies him, for it doth signifie both. It is true that *Tertullian* sayes, *De vacuo similitudo non competit*; If the vision be but a comparison, if there were no such thing as a resurrection, the comparison did not hold. *De nullo parabola non convenit*, saies he, and truly; If there were no resurrection to which that Parable might have relation, it were no Parable. All that is true; but there was a resurrection alwaies knowne to them, alwaies beleeved by them, and that made their present resurrection from that calamity, the more easie, the more intelligible, the more credible, the more discernable to them.

Let therefore Gods method, be thy method; fixe thy self firmly upon that beliefe of the generall resurrection, and thou wilt never doubt of either of the particular resurrections, either from sin, by Gods grace, or from worldly calamities, by Gods power. For that last resurrection is the ground of all. By that *Verè victa mors*, saies *Irenæus*, this last enemy, death, is truly destroyed, because his last spoile, the body, is taken out of his hands. The same body, *eadem ovis*, (as the same Father notes) Christ did not fetch another sheep to the flock, in the place of that which was lost, but the same sheep: God shall not give me another, a better body at the resurrection, but the same body made better; for *Si non haberet caro salvari, neutiquam verbum Dei caro factum fuisset*, If the flesh of man were not to be saved, the Anchor of salvation would never have taken the flesh of man upon him.

The punishment that God laid upon *Adam*, *In dolore & in sudore*, *In sweat, and in sorrow shalt thou eate thy bread*, is but *Donec reverteris*, *till man returne to dust:* but when Man is returned to dust, God returnes

to the remembrance of that promise, *Awake and sing
ye that dwell in the dust*. A mercy already exhibited
to us, in the person of our Saviour Christ Jesus, in
whom, *Per primitias benedixit campo*, (saies S. *Chrysostome*) as God by taking a handfull for the first
Fruits, gave a blessing to the whole field; so he hath
sealed the bodies of all mankind to his glory, by pre-
assuming the body of Christ to that glory. For by
that there is now *Commercium inter Cœlum & terram*;
there is a Trade driven, a Staple established betweene
Heaven and earth; *Ibi caro nostra, hic Spiritus ejus*;
Thither have we sent our flesh, and hither hath he
sent his Spirit.

This is the last abolition of this enemy, Death; for
after this, the bodies of the Saints he cannot touch,
the bodies of the damned he cannot kill, and if he
could, hee were not therein their enemy, but their
friend. This is that blessed and glorious State, of
which, when all the Apostles met to make the Creed,
they could say no more, but *Credo Resurrectionem, I
beleeve the Resurrection of the body*; and when those
two Reverend Fathers, to whom it belongs, shall come
to speake of it, upon the day proper for it, in this
place, and if all the Bishops that ever met in Councels
should meet them here, they could but second the
Apostles *Credo*, with their *Anathema*, We beleeve,
and woe be unto them that doe not beleeve the Resurrection of the body; but in going about to expresse it,
the lips of an Angell would be uncircumcised lips,
and the tongue of an Archangell would stammer. I
offer not therefore at it: but in respect of, and with
relation to that blessed State, according to the doc-
trine, and practise of our Church, we doe pray for the

dead; for the militant Church upon earth, and the triumphant Church in Heaven, and the whole Catholique Church in Heaven, and earth; we doe pray that God will be pleased to hasten that Kingdome, that we with all others departed in the true Faith of his holy Name, may have this perfect consummation, both of body and soule, in his everlasting glory, *Amen*.

SERMON LXVI

Preached at S. Pauls, Ianuary 29, 1625.

PSAL. 63. 7. *Because thou hast been my helpe, Therefore in
the shadow of thy wings will I rejoyce.*

THE Psalmes are the Manna of the Church. As Manna
tasted to every man like that that he liked best, so doe
the Psalmes minister Instruction, and satisfaction, to
every man, in every emergency and occasion. *David*
was not onely a cleare Prophet of Christ himselfe, but
a Prophet of every particular Christian; He foretels
what I, what any shall doe, and suffer, and say. And
as the whole booke of Psalmes is *Oleum effusum*, (as
the Spouse speaks of the name of Christ) an Oynt-
ment powred out upon all sorts of sores, A Searcloth
that souples all bruises, A Balme that searches all
wounds; so are there some certaine Psalmes, that are
Imperiall Psalmes, that command over all affections,
and spread themselves over all occasions, Catholique,
universall Psalmes, that apply themselves to all necessities. This is one of those; for, of those Constitutions
which are called Apostolicall, one is, That the Church
should meet every day, to sing this Psalme. And
accordingly, S. *Chrysostome* testifies, That it was decreed, and ordained by the Primitive Fathers, that no
day should passe without the publique singing of this
Psalme. Under both these obligations, (those ancient
Constitutions, called the Apostles, and those ancient

Decrees made by the primitive Fathers) belongs to
me, who have my part in the service of Gods Church,
the especiall meditation, and recommendation of this
Psalme. And under a third obligation too, That it is
one of those five psalmes, the daily rehearsing whereof,
is injoyned to me, by the Constitutions of this Church,
as five other are to every other person of our body.
As the whole booke is Manna, so these five Psalmes
are my Gomer, which I am to fill and empty every
day of this Manna.

Now as the spirit and soule of the whole booke of
Psalmes is contracted into this psalme, so is the spirit
and soule of this whole psalme contracted into this
verse. The key of the psalme, (as S. *Hierome* calls the
Titles of the psalmes) tells us, that *David* uttered this
psalme, *when he was in the wildernesse of Iudah*; There
we see the present occasion that moved him; And we
see what was passed between God and him before, in
the first clause of our Text; (*Because thou hast been
my helpe*) And then we see what was to come, by the
rest, (*Therefore in the shadow of thy wings will I rejoyce*.) So that we have here the whole compasse of
Time, Past, Present, and Future; and these three
parts of Time, shall be at this time, the three parts of
this Exercise; first, what *Davids* distresse put him
upon for the present; and that lyes in the Context;
secondly, how *David* built his assurance upon that
which was past; (*Because thou hast been my help*) And
thirdly, what he established to himselfe for the future,
(*Therefore in the shadow of thy wings will I rejoyce*.)
First, His distresse in the Wildernesse, his present
estate carried him upon the memory of that which
God had done for him before, And the Remembrance

of that carried him upon that, of which he assured
himselfe after. Fixe upon God any where, and you
shall find him a Circle; He is with you now, when you
fix upon him; He was with you before, for he brought
you to this fixation; and he will be with you hereafter,
for *He is yesterday, and to day, and the same for ever*.

For *Davids* present condition, who was now in a
banishment, in a persecution in the Wildernesse of
Judah, (which is our first part) we shall onely insist
upon that, (which is indeed spread over all the psalme
to the Text, and ratified in the Text) That in all those
temporall calamities *David* was onely sensible of his
spirituall losse; It grieved him not that he was kept
from *Sauls* Court, but that he was kept from Gods
Church. For when he says, by way of lamentation,
*That he was in a dry and thirsty land, where no water
was*, he expresses what penury, what barrennesse,
what drought and what thirst he meant; *To see thy
power, and thy glory, so as I have seene thee in the
Sanctuary*. For there, *my soule shall be satisfied as
with marrow, and with fatnesse*, and there, *my mouth
shall praise thee with joyfull lips*. And in some few
considerations conducing to this. That spirituall
losses are incomparably heavier then temporall, and
that therefore, The Restitution to our spirituall happinesse, or the continuation of it, is rather to be made
the subject of our prayers to God, in all pressures and
distresses, then of temporall, we shall determine that
first part. And for the particular branches of both
the other parts, (The Remembring of Gods benefits
past, And the building of an assurance for the future,
upon that Remembrance) it may be fitter to open
them to you, anon when we come to handle them,

then now. Proceed we now to our first part, The comparing of temporall and spirituall afflictions.

In the way of this Comparison, falls first the Consideration of the universality of afflictions in generall, and the inevitablenesse thereof. It is a blessed Metaphore, that the Holy Ghost hath put into the mouth of the Apostle, *Pondus Gloriæ*, That our *afflictions* are but *light*, because there is an *exceeding*, and an *eternall waight of glory* attending them. If it were not for that exceeding waight of glory, no other waight in this world could turne the scale, or waigh downe those infinite waights of afflictions that oppresse us here. There is not onely *Pestis valde gravis*, (*the pestilence grows heavy upon the Land*) but there is *Musca valde gravis*, God calls in but the fly, to vexe Egypt, and even the fly is a heavy burden unto them. It is not onely *Iob* that complains, *That he was a burden to himselfe*, but even *Absaloms* haire was a burden to him, till it was polled. It is not onely *Ieremy* that complains, *Aggravavit compedes*, That God had made their fetters and their chains heavy to them, but the workmen in harvest complaine, That God had made a faire day heavy unto them, (*We have borne the heat, and the burden of the day*.) *Sand is heavy*, sayes *Solomon*; And how many suffer so? under a sand-hill of crosses, daily, hourely afflictions, that are heavy by their number, if not by their single waight? And *a stone is heavy*; (sayes he in the same place) And how many suffer so? How many, without any former preparatory crosse, or comminatory, or commonitory crosse, even in the midst of prosperity, and security, fall under some one stone, some grind-stone, some mil-stone, some one insupportable crosse that ruines them? But then, (sayes *Solomon* there) *A fooles anger is heavier then both*; And how many children, and servants, and wives suffer under the anger, and morosity, and peevishnesse, and jealousie of foolish Masters, and Parents, and Husbands, though they must not say so? *David* and *Solomon* have cryed out, That all this world is *vanity*, and *levity*; And (God knowes) all is waight, and burden, and heavinesse, and oppression; And if there were not a waight of future glory to counterpoyse it, we should all sinke into nothing.

I aske not *Mary Magdalen*, whether lightnesse were not a burden; (for sin is certainly, sensibly a burden) But I aske *Susanna* whether even chast beauty were not a burden to her; and I aske *Ioseph* whether personall comelinesse were not a burden to him. I aske not *Dives*, who perished in the next world, the question; but I aske them who are made examples of *Solomons* Rule, of that *sore evill*, (as he calls it) *Riches kept to the owners thereof for their hurt*, whether Riches be not a burden.

All our life is a continuall burden, yet we must not groane; A continuall squeasing, yet we must not pant; And as in the tendernesse of our childhood, we suffer, and yet are whipt if we cry, so we are complained of, if we complaine, and made delinquents if we call the times ill. And that which addes waight to waight, and multiplies the sadnesse of this consideration, is this, That still the best men have had most laid upon them. As soone as I heare God say, that he hath found *an upright man*, *that feares God*, *and eschews evill*, in the next lines I finde a Commission to Satan, to bring in Sabeans and Chaldeans upon his cattell, and servants, and fire and tempest upon his children, and loathsome diseases upon himselfe. As soone as I heare God say, That he hath found *a man according to his own heart*, I see his sonnes ravish his daughters, and then murder one another, and then rebell against the Father, and put him into straites for his life. As soone as I heare God testifie of Christ at his Baptisme, *This is my beloved Sonne in whom I am well pleased*, I finde that Sonne of his *led up by the Spirit, to be tempted of the Devill*. And after I heare God ratifie the same testimony againe, at his Transfiguration, (*This is my beloved Sonne, in whom I am well pleased*) I finde that beloved Sonne of his, deserted, abandoned, and given over to Scribes, and Pharisees, and Publicans, and Herodians, and Priests, and Souldiers, and people, and Judges, and witnesses, and executioners, and he that was called the beloved Sonne of God, and made partaker of the glory of heaven, in this world, in his Transfiguration, is made now the Sewer of all the corruption, of all the sinnes of this world, as no Sonne of God, but a meere man, as no man, but a contemptible worme. As though the greatest weaknesse in this world, were man, and the greatest fault in man were to be good, man is more miserable then other creatures, and good men more miserable then any other men.

But then there is *Pondus Gloriæ, An exceeding waight of eternall glory*, and that turnes the scale; for as it makes all worldly prosperity as dung, so it makes all worldly adversity as feathers. And so it had need; for in the scale against it, there are not onely put temporall afflictions, but spirituall too; And to these two kinds, we may accommodate those words, *He*

that fals upon this stone, (upon temporall afflictions)
may be bruised, broken, *But he upon whom that stone
falls*, (spirituall afflictions) *is in danger to be ground to
powder*. And then, the great, and yet ordinary danger
is, That these spirituall afflictions grow out of temporall; Murmuring, and diffidence in God, and obduration, out of worldly calamities; And so against
nature, the fruit is greater and heavier then the Tree,
spirituall heavier then temporall afflictions.

They who write of Naturall story, propose that
Plant for the greatest wonder in nature, which being
no firmer then a bull-rush, or a reed, produces and
beares for the fruit thereof no other but an intire, and
very hard stone. That temporall affliction should produce spirituall stoninesse, and obduration, is un-
naturall, yet ordinary. Therefore doth God propose
it, as one of those greatest blessings, which he multiplies upon his people, *I will take away your stony
hearts, and give you hearts of flesh*; And, Lord let mee
have a fleshly heart in any sense, rather then a stony
heart. Wee finde mention amongst the observers of
rarities in Nature, of hairy hearts, hearts of men, that
have beene overgrowne with haire; but of petrified
hearts, hearts of men growne into stone, we read not;
for this petrefaction of the heart, this stupefaction of
a man, is the last blow of Gods hand upon the heart
of man in this world. Those great afflictions which are
powred out of the Vials of the seven Angels upon the
world, are still accompanied with that heavy effect,
that that affliction hardned them. *They were scorched
with heats and plagues*, by the fourth Angel, and it
followes, *They blasphemed the name of God, and repented not, to give him glory*. Darknesse was induced

upon them by the fift Angel, and it followes, *They blasphemed the God of heaven, and repented not of their deeds*. And from the seventh Angel there fell haile-stones of the waight of talents, (perchance foure pound waight) upon men; And yet these men had so much life left, as to *blaspheme God*, out of that respect, which alone should have brought them to glorifie God, *Because the plague thereof was exceeding great*. And when a great plague brings them to blaspheme, how great shall that second plague be, that comes upon them for blaspheming?

Let me wither and weare out mine age in a discomfortable, in an unwholesome, in a penurious prison, and so pay my debts with my bones, and recompence the wastfulnesse of my youth, with the beggery of mine age; Let me wither in a spittle under sharpe, and foule, and infamous diseases, and so recompence the wantonnesse of my youth, with that loathsomnesse in mine age; yet, if God with-draw not his spirituall blessings, his Grace, his Patience, If I can call my suffering his Doing, my passion his Action, All this that is temporall, is but a caterpiller got into one corner of my garden, but a mill-dew fallen upon one acre of my Corne; The body of all, the substance of all is safe, as long as the soule is safe. But when I shall trust to that, which wee call a good spirit, and God shall deject, and empoverish, and evacuate that spirit, when I shall rely upon a morall constancy, and God shall shake, and enfeeble, and enervate, destroy and demolish that constancy; when I shall think to refresh my selfe in the serenity and sweet ayre of a good conscience, and God shall call up the damps and vapours of hell it selfe, and spread a cloud of diffi-

dence, and an impenetrable crust of desperation upon
my conscience; when health shall flie from me, and
I shall lay hold upon riches to succour me, and comfort me in my sicknesse, and riches shall flie from me,
and I shall snatch after favour, and good opinion, to
comfort me in my poverty; when even this good
opinion shall leave me, and calumnies and misinfor-
mations shall prevaile against me; when I shall need
peace, because there is none but thou, O Lord, that
should stand for me, and then shall finde, that all the
wounds that I have, come from thy hand, all the
arrowes that stick in me, from thy quiver; when I
shall see, that because I have given my selfe to my
corrupt nature, thou hast changed thine; and because
I am all evill towards thee, therefore thou hast given
over being good towards me; When it comes to this
height, that the fever is not in the humors, but in the
spirits, that mine enemy is not an imaginary enemy,
fortune, nor a transitory enemy, malice in great persons, but a reall, and an irresistible, and an inexorable,
and an everlasting enemy, The Lord of Hosts himselfe, The Almighty God himselfe, the Almighty God
himselfe onely knowes the waight of this affliction,
and except hee put in that *pondus gloriæ*, that exceeding
waight of an eternall glory, with his owne hand, into
the other scale, we are waighed downe, we are
swallowed up, irreparably, irrevocably, irrecoverably,
irremediably.

This is the fearefull depth, this is spirituall misery,
to be thus fallen from God. But was this *Davids* case?
was he fallen thus farre, into a diffidence in God?
No. But the danger, the precipice, the slippery sliding
into that bottomlesse depth, is, to be excluded from

the meanes of comming to God, or staying with God;
And this is that that *David* laments here, That by
being banished, and driven into the wildernesse of
Judah, hee had not accesse to the Sanctuary of the
Lord, to sacrifice his part in the praise, and to receive
his part in the prayers of the Congregation; for Angels
passe not to ends, but by wayes and meanes, nor men
to the glory of the triumphant Church, but by par-
ticipation of the Communion of the Militant. To this
note *David* sets his Harpe, in many, many Psalms:
Sometimes, that God had suffered his enemies to
possesse his Tabernacle, (*Hee forsooke the Tabernacle
of Shiloh, Hee delivered his strength into captivity, and
his glory into the enemies hands*) But most commonly
he complaines, that God disabled him from comming
to the Sanctuary. In which one thing he had summed
up all his desires, all his prayers, (*One thing have I
desired of the Lord, that will I looke after; That I may
dwell in the house of the Lord, all the dayes of my life,
to behold the beauty of the Lord, and to enquire in his
Temple*) His vehement desire of this, he expresses
againe, (*My soule thirsteth for God, for the living God;
when shall I come and appeare before God?*) He expresses a holy jealousie, a religious envy, even to the
sparrows and swallows, (yea, *the sparrow hath found
a house, and the swallow a nest for her selfe, and where
she may lay her yong, Even thine Altars, O Lord of
Host, my King and my God*.) Thou art my King, and
my God, and yet excludest me from that, which thou
affordest to sparrows, *And are not we of more value
then many sparrows?*

And as though *David* felt some false ease, some
half-tentation, some whispering that way, That God

is *in the wildernesse of Iudah*, in every place, as well
as in his *Sanctuary*, there is in the Originall in that
place, a patheticall, a vehement, a broken expressing
expressed, *O thine Altars*; It is true, (sayes *David*)
thou art here in the wildernesse, and I may see thee
here, and serve thee here, but, *O thine Altars, O Lord
of hosts, my King and my God*. When *David* could not
come in person to that place, yet he bent towards the
Temple, (*In thy feare will I worship towards thy holy
Temple*.) Which was also *Daniels* devotion; when he
prayed, *his Chamber windowes were open towards Ierusalem*; And so is *Hezekias* turning to the wall to weepe,
and to pray in his sick bed, understood to be to that
purpose, to conforme, and compose himselfe towards
the Temple. In the place consecrated for that use,
God by *Moses* fixes the service, and fixes the Reward;
And towards that place, (when they could not come
to it) doth *Solomon* direct their devotion in the Con-
secration of the Temple, (*when they are in the warres,
when they are in Captivity, and pray towards this house,
doe thou heare them*.) For, as in private prayer, when
(according to Christs command) we are shut in our
chamber, there is exercised *Modestia fidei*, The
modesty and bashfulnesse of our faith, not pressing
upon God in his house: so in the publique prayers of
the Congregation, there is exercised the fervor, and
holy courage of our faith, for *Agmine facto obsidemus
Deum*, It is a Mustering of our forces, and a besieging
of God. Therefore does *David* so much magnifie their
blessednesse, that are in this house of God; (*Blessed are
they that dwell in thy house, for they will be still praising
thee*) Those that looke towards it, may praise thee
sometimes, but those men who dwell in the Church,

and whose whole service lyes in the Church, have certainly an advantage of all other men (who are necessarily withdrawne by worldly businesses) in making themselves acceptable to almighty God, if they doe their duties, and observe their Church-services aright.

Man being therefore thus subject naturally to manifold calamities, and spirituall calamities being incomparably heavier then temporall, and the greatest danger of falling into such spirituall calamities being in our absence from Gods Church, where onely the outward meanes of happinesse are ministred unto us, certainely there is much tendernesse and deliberation to be used, before the Church doores be shut against any man. If I would not direct a prayer to God, to excommunicate any man from the Triumphant Church, (which were to damne him) I would not oyle the key, I would not make the way too slippery for excommunications in the Militant Church; For, that is to endanger him. I know how distastfull a sin to God, contumacy, and contempt, and disobedience to Order and Authority is; And I know, (and all men, that choose not ignorance, may know) that our Excommunications (though calumniators impute them to small things, because, many times, the first complaint is of some small matter) never issue but upon contumacies, contempts, disobediences to the Church. But they are reall contumacies, not interpretative, apparant contumacies, not presumptive, that excommunicate a man in Heaven; And much circumspection is required, and (I am far from doubting it) exercised in those cases upon earth; for, though every Excommunication upon earth be not sealed in Heaven, though it damne not the man, yet it dammes up that mans way, by shutting him out of that Church, through which he must goe to the other; which being so great a danger, let every man take heed of Excommunicating himselfe. The imperswasible Recusant does so; The negligent Libertin does so; The fantastique Separatist does so; The halfe-present man, he, whose body is here, and minde away, does so; And he, whose body is but halfe here, his limbes are here upon a cushion, but his eyes, his eares are not here, does so: All these are selfe-Excommunicators, and keepe themselves from hence. Onely he enjoyes that blessing, the want whereof *David* deplores, that is here intirely, and is glad he is here, and glad to finde this kinde of service here, that he does, and wishes no other.

And so we have done with our first Part, *Davids* aspect, his present condition, and his danger of falling into spirituall miserles, because his persecution, and banishment amounted to an Excommunication, to an excluding of him from the service of God, in the Church. And we passe, in our Order proposed at first, to the second, his retrospect, the Consideration, what God had done for him before, *Because thou hast beene my helpe.*

Through this second part, we shall passe by these three steps. First, That it behoves us, in all our purposes, and actions, to propose to our selves a copy to write by, a patterne to worke by, a rule, or an example to proceed by, Because it hath beene thus heretofore, sayes *David*, I will resolve upon this course for the future. And secondly, That the copy, the patterne, the precedent which we are to propose to our selves,

is, The observation of Gods former wayes and proceedings upon us, Because God hath already gone
this way, this way I will awaite his going still. And
then, thirdly and lastly, in this second part, The way
that God had formerly gone with *David*, which was,
That he had been his helpe, (*Because thou hast beene
my helpe.*)

First then, from the meanest artificer, through the
wisest Philosopher, to God himselfe, all that is well
done, or wisely undertaken, is undertaken and done
according to pre-conceptions, fore-imaginations, de-
signes, and patterns proposed to our selves beforehand.
A Carpenter builds not a house, but that he first sets
up a frame in his owne minde, what kinde of house
he will build. The little great Philosopher *Epictetus*,
would undertake no action, but he would first propose
to himselfe, what *Socrates*, or *Plato*, what a wise man
would do in that case, and according to that, he would
proceed. Of God himselfe, it is safely resolved in the
Schoole, that he never did any thing in any part of
time, of which he had not an eternal pre-conception,
an eternall Idea, in himselfe before. Of which Ideaes,
that is, pre-conceptions, pre-determinations in God,
S. *Augustine* pronounces, *Tanta vis in Ideis consti-
tuitur*, There is so much truth, and so much power in
these Ideaes, as that without acknowledging them, no
man can acknowledge God, for he does not allow God
Counsaile, and Wisdome, and deliberation in his
Actions, but sets God on worke, before he have
thought what he will doe. And therefore he, and
others of the Fathers read that place, (which we read
otherwise) *Quod factum est, in ipso vita erat*; that is,
in all their Expositions, whatsoever is made, in time,

was alive in God, before it was made, that is, in that
eternall Idea, and patterne which was in him. So also
doe divers of those Fathers read those words to the
Hebrews, (which we read, *The things that are seene,
are not made of things that doe appeare*) *Ex invisibilibus
visibilia facta sunt, Things formerly invisible, were made
visible*; that is, we see them not till now, till they are
made, but they had an invisible being, in that Idea,
in that pre-notion, in that purpose of God before, for
ever before. Of all things in Heaven, and earth, but
of himselfe, God had an Idea, a patterne in himselfe,
before he made it.

And therefore let him be our patterne for that, to
worke after patternes; To propose to our selves Rules
and Examples for all our actions; and the more, the
more immediately, the more directly our actions concerne the service of God. If I aske God, by what
Idea he made me, God produces his *Faciamus hominem
ad Imaginem nostram*, That there was a concurrence
of the whole Trinity, to make me in *Adam*, according
to that Image which they were, and according to that
Idea, which they had pre-determined. If I pretend
to serve God, and he aske me for my Idea, How I
meane to serve him, shall I bee able to produce none?
If he aske me an Idea of my Religion, and my opinions,
shall I not be able to say, It is that which thy word,
and thy Catholique Church hath imprinted in me?
If he aske me an Idea of my prayers, shall I not be
able to say, It is that which my particular necessities,
that which the forme prescribed by thy Son, that
which the care, and piety of the Church, in con-
ceiving fit prayers, hath imprinted in me? If he aske
me an Idea of my Sermons, shall I not be able to say,

It is that which the Analogy of Faith, the edification of the Congregation, the zeale of thy worke, the meditations of my heart have imprinted in me? But if I come to pray or to preach without this kind of Idea, if I come to extemporall prayer, and extemporall preaching, I shall come to an extemporall faith, and extemporall religion; and then I must looke for an extemporall Heaven, a Heaven to be made for me; for to that Heaven which belongs to the Catholique Church, I shall never come, except I go by the way of the Catholique Church, by former Idea's, former examples, former patterns, To beleeve according to ancient beliefes, to pray according to ancient formes, to preach according to former meditations. God does nothing, man does nothing well, without these Idea's, these retrospects, this recourse to pre-conceptions, pre-deliberations.

Something then I must propose to my selfe, to be the rule, and the reason of my present and future actions; which was our first branch in this second Part; And then the second is, That I can propose nothing more availably, then the contemplation of the history of Gods former proceeding with me; which is *Davids* way here, Because this was Gods way before, I will looke for God in this way still. That language in which God spake to ´man, the Hebrew, hath no present tense; They forme not their verbs as our Westerne Languages do, in the present, *I heare*, or *I see*, or *I reade*, But they begin at that which is past, *I have seene* and *heard*, and *read*. God carries us in his Language, in his speaking, upon that which is past, upon that which he hath done already; I cannot have better security for present, nor future, then Gods former mercies exhibited to me. *Quis non gaudeat*, sayes S. *Augustine*, Who does not triumph with joy, when hee considers what God hath done? *Quis non & ea, quæ nondum venerunt, ventura sperat, propter illa, quæ jam tanta impleta sunt?* Who can doubt of the performance of all, that sees the greatest part of a Prophesie performed? If I have found that true that God hath said, of the person of Antichrist, why should I doubt of that which he sayes of the ruine of Antichrist? *Credamus modicum quod restat*, sayes the same Father, It is much that wee have seene done, and it is but little that God hath reserved to our faith, to beleeve that it shall be done.

There is no State, no Church, no Man, that hath not this tie upon God, that hath not God in these bands, That God by having done much for them already, hath bound himselfe to doe more. Men proceed in their former wayes, sometimes, lest they should confesse an error, and acknowledge that they had beene in a wrong way. God is obnoxious to no error, and therefore he does still, as he did before. Every one of you can say now to God, Lord, Thou broughtest me hither, therefore enable me to heare; Lord, Thou doest that, therefore make me understand; And that, therefore let me beleeve; And that too, therefore strengthen me to the practise; And all that, therefore continue me to a perseverance. Carry it up to the first sense and apprehension that ever thou hadst of Gods working upon thee, either in thy selfe, when thou camest first to the use of reason, or in others in thy behalfe, in thy baptisme, yet when thou thinkest thou art at the first, God had done something for thee before all that; before that, hee had elected thee, in that election which S. *Augustine* speaks of, *Habet electos, quos creaturus est eligendos*, God hath elected certaine men, whom he intends to create, that he may elect them; that is, that he may declare his Election upon them. God had thee, before he made thee; He loved thee first, and then created thee, that thou loving him, he might continue his love to thee. The surest way, and the nearest way to lay hold upon God, is the consideration of that which he had done already. So *David* does; And that which he takes knowledge of, in particular, in Gods former proceedings towards him, is, Because God had been his helpe, which is our last branch in this part, *Because thou hast beene my helpe.*

From this one word, That God hath been my *Helpe*, I make account that we have both these notions; first, That God hath not left me to my selfe, He hath come to my succour, He hath helped me; And then, That God hath not left out my selfe; He hath been my Helpe, but he hath left some thing for me to doe with him, and by his helpe. My security for the future, in this consideration of that which is past, lyes not onely in this, That God hath delivered me, but in this also, that he hath delivered me by way of a Helpe, and Helpe alwayes presumes an endevour and co-operation in him that is helped. God did not elect me as a helper, nor create me, nor redeeme me, nor convert me, by way of helping me; for he alone did all, and he had no use at all of me. God infuses his first grace, the first way, meerly as a Giver; intirely, all himselfe; but his subsequent graces, as a helper; therefore we call them Auxiliant graces, Helping graces; and we alwayes receive them, when we

endevour to make use of his former grace. *Lord, I
beleeve*, (sayes the Man in the Gospel to Christ) *Helpe
mine unbeliefe*. If there had not been unbeliefe, weaknesse, unperfectnesse in that faith, there had needed
no helpe; but if there had not been a Beliefe, a faith,
it had not been capable of helpe and assistance, but
it must have been an intire act, without any concurrence on the mans part.

So that if I have truly the testimony of a rectified
Conscience, That God hath helped me, it is in both
respects; first, That he hath never forsaken me, and
then, That he hath never suffered me to forsake my
selfe; He hath blessed me with that grace, that I trust
in no helpe but his, and with this grace too, That I
cannot looke for his helpe, except I helpe my selfe
also. God did not helpe heaven and earth to proceed
out of nothing in the Creation, for they had no possi-
bility of any disposition towards it; for they had no
beeing: But God did helpe the earth to produce grasse,
and herbes; for, for that, God had infused a seminall
disposition into the earth, which, for all that, it could
not have perfected without his farther helpe. As in
the making of Woman, there is the very word of our
Text, *Gnazar*, God made him a *Helper*, one that was
to doe much for him, but not without him. So that
then, if I will make Gods former working upon me,
an argument of his future gracious purposes, as I
must acknowledge that God hath done much for me,
so I must finde, that I have done what I could, by
the benefit of that grace with him; for God promises
to be but a helper. *Lord open thou my lips*, sayes *David*;
that is Gods worke intirely; And then, *My mouth, My
mouth shall shew forth thy praise*; there enters *David*

into the worke with God. And then, sayes God to him, *Dilata os tuum, Open thy mouth*, (It is now made *Thy mouth*, and therefore doe thou open it) *and I will fill it*; All inchoations and consummations, beginnings and perfectings are of God, of God alone; but in the way there is a concurrence on our part, (by a successive continuation of Gods grace) in which God proceeds as a Helper; and I put him to more then that, if I doe nothing. But if I pray for his helpe, and apprehend and husband his graces well, when they come, then he is truly, properly my helper; and upon that security, that testimony of a rectified Conscience, I can proceed to *Davids* confidence for the future, *Because thou hast been my Helpe, therefore in the shadow of thy wings will I rejoyce*; which is our third, and last generall part.

In this last part, which is, (after *Davids* aspect, and consideration of his present condition, which was, in the effect, an Exclusion from Gods Temple, And his retrospect, his consideration of Gods former mercies to him, That he had been his Helpe) his prospect, his confidence for the future, we shall stay a little upon these two steps; first, That that which he promises himselfe, is not an immunity from all powerfull enemies, nor a sword of revenge upon those enemies; It is not that he shall have no adversary, nor that that adversary shall be able to doe him no harme, but that he should have a refreshing, a respiration, *In velamento alarum*, under the shadow of Gods wings. And then, (in the second place) That this way which God shall be pleased to take, this manner, this measure of refreshing, which God shall vouchsafe to afford, (though it amount not to a full deliverance) must produce a joy, a rejoycing in us; we must not onely not decline to a murmuring, that we have no more, no nor rest upon a patience for that which remains, but we must ascend to a holy joy, as if all were done and accomplished, *In the shadow of thy wings will I rejoyce*.

First then, lest any man in his dejection of spirit, or of fortune, should stray into a jealousie or suspition of Gods power to deliver him, As God hath spangled the firmament with starres, so hath he his Scriptures with names, and Metaphors, and denotations of power. Sometimes he shines out in the name of a *Sword*, and of a *Target*, and of a *Wall*, and of a *Tower*, and of a *Rocke*, and of a *Hill*; And sometimes in that glorious and manifold constellation of all together, *Dominus exercituum, The Lord of Hosts*. God, as God, is never represented to us, with Defensive Armes; He needs them not. When the Poets present their great Heroes, and their Worthies, they always insist upon their Armes, they spend much of their invention upon the description of their Armes; both because the greatest valour and strength needs Armes, (*Goliah* himselfe was armed) and because to expose ones selfe to danger unarmed, is not valour, but rashnesse. But God is invulnerable in himselfe, and is never represented armed; you finde no shirts of mayle, no Helmets, no Cuirasses in Gods Armory. In that one place of *Esay*, where it may seeme to be otherwise, where God is said *to have put on righteousnesse as a breastplate, and a Helmet of salvation upon his head*; in that prophecy God is Christ, and is therefore in that place, called *the Redeemer*. Christ needed defensive armes, God does not. Gods word does; His Scriptures doe; And therefore S. *Hierome* hath armed them, and set before every booke his *Prologum gale-atum*, that prologue that armes and defends every booke from calumny. But though God need not, nor receive not defensive armes for himselfe, yet God is to us a Helmet, a Breastplate, a strong tower, a rocke, every thing that may give us assurance and defence; and as often as he will, he can refresh that Proclamation, *Nolite tangere Christos meos*, Our enemies shall not so much as touch us.

But here, by occasion of his Metaphore in this Text, (*Sub umbra alarum*, *In the shadow of thy wings*) we doe not so much consider an absolute immunity, That we shall not be touched, as a refreshing and consolation, when we are touched, though we be pinched and wounded. The Names of God, which are most frequent in the Scriptures, are these three, *Elohim*, and *Adonai*, and *Iehovah*; and to assure us of his Power to deliver us, two of these three are Names of Power. *Elohim* is *Deus fortis*, The mighty, The powerfull God: And (which deserves a particular consideration) *Elohim* is a plurall Name; It is not *Deus fortis*, but *Dii fortes*, powerfull Gods. God is all kinde of Gods; All kinds, which either Idolaters and Gentils can imagine, (as Riches, or Justice, or Wisdome, or Valour, or such) and all kinds which God himself hath called gods, (as Princes, and Magistrates, and Prelates, and all that assist and helpe one another) God is *Elohim*, All these Gods, and all these in their height and best of their power; for *Elohim*, is *Dii fortes*, Gods in the plurall, and those plurall gods in their exaltation.

The second Name of God, is a Name of power too, *Adonai*. For, *Adonai* is *Dominus*, The Lord, such a

Lord, as is Lord and Proprietary of all his creatures,
and all creatures are his creatures; And then, *Do-
minium est potestas tum utendi, tum abutendi*, sayes the
law; To be absolute Lord of any thing, gives that
Lord a power to doe what he will with that thing.
God, as he is *Adonai, The Lord*, may give and take,
quicken and kill, build and throw downe, where and
whom he will. So then two of Gods three Names are
Names of absolute power, to imprint, and re-imprint
an assurance in us, that hee can absolutely deliver us,
and fully revenge us, if he will. But then, his third
Name, and that Name which hee chooses to himselfe,
and in the signification of which Name, hee employes
Moses, for the reliefe of his people under Pharaoh,
that Name *Iehovah*, is not a Name of Power, but onely
of Essence, of Being, of Subsistence, and yet in the
vertue of that Name, God relieved his people. And
if, in my afflictions, God vouchsafe to visit mee in
that Name, to preserve me in my being, in my subsistence in him, that I be not shaked out of him, dis-
inherited in him, excommunicate from him, devested
of him, annihilated towards him, let him, at his good
pleasure, reserve his *Elohim*, and his *Adonai*, the
exercises and declarations of his mighty Power, to
those great publike causes, that more concerne his
Glory, then any thing that can befall me; But if he
impart his *Iehovah*, enlarge himselfe so far towards
me, as that I may live, and move, & have my beeing
in him, though I be not instantly delivered, nor mine
enemies absolutely destroyed, yet this is as much as
I should promise my selfe, this is as much as the
Holy Ghost intends in this Metaphor, *Sub umbra
alarum, Vnder the shadow of thy wings*, that is a Re-

freshing, a Respiration, a Conservation, a Consolation in all afflictions that are inflicted upon me.

Yet, is not this Metaphor of *Wings* without a denotation of Power. As no Act of Gods, though it seeme to imply but spirituall comfort, is without a denotation of power, (for it is the power of God that comforts me; To overcome that sadnesse of soule, and that dejection of spirit, which the Adversary by temporall afflictions would induce upon me, is an act of his Power) So this Metaphor, *The shadow of his wings*, (which in this place expresses no more, then consolation and refreshing in misery, and not a powerfull deliverance out of it) is so often in the Scriptures made a denotation of Power too, as that we can doubt of no act of power, if we have this shadow of his wings. For, in this Metaphor of *Wings*, doth the Holy Ghost expresse the *Maritime* power, the power of some Nations at Sea, in Navies, (*Woe to the land shadowing with wings*;) that is, that hovers over the world, and intimidates it with her sailes and ships. In this Metaphor doth God remember his people, of his powerfull deliverance of them, (*You have seene what I did unto the Egyptians, and how I bare you on Eagles wings, and brought you to my selfe*.) In this Metaphor doth God threaten his and their enemies, what hee can doe, (*The noise of the wings of his Cherubims, are as the noise of great waters, and of an Army*.) So also, what hee will doe, (*Hee shall spread his wings over Bozrah, and at that day shall the hearts of the mighty men of Edom, be as the heart of a woman in her pangs*.) So that, if I have the shadow of his wings, I have the earnest of the power of them too; If I have refreshing, and respiration from them, I am able to say, (as those three Confessors did to *Nebu-chadnezzar*) *My God is able to deliver me*, I am sure he hath power; *And my God will deliver me*, when it conduces to his glory, I know he will; *But, if he doe not, bee it knowne unto thee, O King, we will not serve thy Gods*; Be it knowne unto thee, O Satan, how long soever God deferre my deliverance, I will not seeke false comforts, the miserable comforts of this world. I will not, for I need not; for I can subsist under this shadow of these Wings, though I have no more.

The Mercy-seat it selfe was covered with the Cherubims Wings; and who would have more then Mercy? and a Mercy-seat; that is, established, resident Mercy, permanent and perpetuall Mercy; present and familiar Mercy; a Mercy-seat. Our Saviour Christ intends as much as would have served their turne, if they had laid hold upon it, when hee says, *That hee would have gathered Ierusalem, as a henne gathers her chickens under her wings.* And though the other Prophets doe (as ye have heard) mingle the signification of Power, and actuall deliverance, in this Metaphor of Wings, yet our Prophet, whom wee have now in especiall consideration, *David*, never doth so; but in every place where hee uses this Metaphor of Wings (which are in five or sixe severall Psalmes) still hee rests and determines in that sense, which is his meaning here; That though God doe not actually deliver us, nor actually destroy our enemies, yet if hee refresh us in the shadow of his Wings, if he maintaine our subsistence (which is a religious Constancy) in him, this should not onely establish our patience, (for that is but halfe the worke) but it should also produce a joy, and rise to an exultation, which is our last circumstance, *Therefore in the shadow of thy wings, I will rejoice*.

I would always raise your hearts, and dilate your hearts, to a holy Joy, to a joy in the Holy Ghost. There may be a just feare, that men doe not grieve enough for their sinnes; but there may bee a just jealousie, and suspition too, that they may fall into inordinate griefe, and diffidence of Gods mercy; And God hath reserved us to such times, as being the later times, give us even the dregs and lees of misery to drinke. For, God hath not onely let loose into the world a new spirituall disease; which is, an equality, and an indifferency, which religion our children, or our servants, or our companions professe; (I would not keepe company with a man that thought me a knave, or a traitor; with him that thought I loved not my Prince, or were a faithlesse man, not to be beleeved, I would not associate my selfe; And yet I will make him my bosome companion, and thinks I doe not love God, that thinks I cannot be saved) but God hath accompanied, and complicated almost all our bodily diseases of these times, with an extraordinary sadnesse, a predominant melancholy, a faintnesse of heart, a chearlesnesse, a joylesnesse of spirit, and therefore I returne often to this endeavor of raising your hearts, dilating your hearts with a holy Joy, Joy in the holy Ghost, for *Vnder the shadow of his wings*, you may, you should *rejoyce*.

If you looke upon this world in a Map, you find two Hemisphears, two half worlds. If you crush heaven into a Map, you may find two Hemisphears too, two half heavens; Halfe will be Joy, and halfe will be Glory; for in these two, the joy of heaven, and

the glory of heaven, is all heaven represented unto us.
And as of those two Hemisphears of the world, the
first hath been knowne long before, but the other,
(that of America, which is the richer in treasure) God
reserved for later Discoveries; So though he reserve
that Hemisphear of heaven, which is the Glory thereof, to the Resurrection, yet the other Hemisphear, the
Joy of heaven, God opens to our Discovery, and de-
livers for our habitation even whilst we dwell in this
world. As God hath cast upon the unrepentant sinner
two deaths, a temporall, and a spirituall death, so hath
he breathed into us two lives; for so, as the word for
death is doubled, *Morte morieris, Thou shalt die the
death*, so is the word for life expressed in the plurall,
*Chaiim, vitarum, God breathed into his nostrils the
breath of lives*, of divers lives. Though our naturall
life were no life, but rather a continuall dying, yet
we have two lives besides that, an eternall life reserved
for heaven, but yet a heavenly life too, a spirituall life,
even in this world; And as God doth thus inflict two
deaths, and infuse two lives, so doth he also passe two
Judgements upon man, or rather repeats the same
Judgement twice. For, that which Christ shall say to
thy soule then at the last Judgement, *Enter into thy
Masters joy*, Hee sayes to thy conscience now, *Enter
into thy Masters joy*. The everlastingnesse of the joy
is the blessednesse of the next life, but the entring,
the inchoation is afforded here. For that which Christ
shall say then to us, *Venite benedicti, Come ye blessed*,
are words intended to persons that are comming, that
are upon the way, though not at home; Here in this
world he bids us *Come*, there in the next, he shall bid
us *Welcome*. The Angels of heaven have joy in thy

conversion, and canst thou bee without that joy in
thy selfe? If thou desire revenge upon thine enemies,
as they are Gods enemies, That God would bee
pleased to remove, and root out all such as oppose
him, that Affection appertaines to Glory; Let that
alone till thou come to the Hemisphear of Glory;
There joyne with those Martyrs under the Altar,
Vsquequo Domine, How long O Lord, dost thou deferre Judgement? and thou shalt have thine answere
there for that. Whilst thou art here, here joyne with
David, and the other Saints of God, in that holy
increpation of a dangerous sadnesse, *Why art thou
cast downe O my soule? why art thou disquieted in mee?*
That soule that is dissected and anatomized to God,
in a sincere confession, washed in the teares of true
contrition, embalmed in the blood of reconciliation,
the blood of Christ Jesus, can assigne no reason, can
give no just answer to that Interrogatory, *Why art
thou cast downe O my soule? why art thou disquieted in
me?* No man is so little, as that he can be lost under
these wings, no man so great, as that they cannot
reach to him; *Semper ille major est, quantumcumque
creverimus*, To what temporall, to what spirituall
greatnesse soever wee grow, still pray wee him to
shadow us under his Wings; for the poore need those
wings against oppression, and the rich against envy.
The Holy Ghost, who is a Dove, shadowed the whole
world under his wings; *Incubabat aquis*, He hovered
over the waters, he sate upon the waters, and he
hatched all that was produced, and all that was produced so, was good. Be thou a Mother where the
Holy Ghost would be a Father; Conceive by him;
and be content that he produce joy in thy heart here.

First thinke, that as a man must have some land, or
els he cannot be in wardship, so a man must have
some of the love of God, or els he could not fall under
Gods correction; God would not give him his physick,
God would not study his cure, if he cared not for him.
And then thinke also, that if God afford thee the
shadow of his wings, that is, Consolation, respiration,
refreshing, though not a present, and plenary deliverance, in thy afflictions, not to thanke God, is a murmuring, and not to rejoyce in Gods wayes, is an
unthankfulnesse. Howling is the noyse of hell, singing the voyce of heaven; Sadnesse the damp of Hell,
Rejoycing the serenity of Heaven. And he that hath
not this joy here, lacks one of the best pieces of his
evidence for the joyes of heaven; and hath neglected
or refused that Earnest, by which God uses to binde
his bargaine, that true joy in this world shall flow into
the joy of Heaven, as a River flowes into the Sea; This
joy shall not be put out in death, and a new joy kindled
in me in Heaven; But as my soule, as soone as it is
out of my body, is in Heaven, and does not stay for
the possession of Heaven, nor for the fruition of the
sight of God, till it be ascended through ayre, and
fire, and Moone, and Sun, and Planets, and Firmament, to that place which we conceive to be Heaven,
but without the thousandth part of a minutes stop,
as soone as it issues, is in a glorious light, which is
Heaven, (for all the way to Heaven is Heaven; And
as those Angels, which came from Heaven hither,
bring Heaven with them, and are in Heaven here, So
that soule that goes to Heaven, meets Heaven here;
and as those Angels doe not devest Heaven by comming, so these soules invest Heaven, in their going.)

As my soule shall not goe towards Heaven, but goe
by Heaven to Heaven, to the Heaven of Heavens, So
the true joy of a good soule in this world is the very
joy of Heaven; and we goe thither, not that being
without joy, we might have joy infused into us, but
that as Christ sayes, *Our joy might be full*, perfected,
sealed with an everlastingnesse; for, as he promises,
That no man shall take our joy from us, so neither shall
Death it selfe take it away, nor so much as interrupt it,
or discontinue it, But as in the face of Death, when he
layes hold upon me, and in the face of the Devill,
when he attempts me, I shall see the face of God,
(for, every thing shall be a glasse, to reflect God upon
me) so in the agonies of Death, in the anguish of that
dissolution, in the sorrowes of that valediction, in the
irreversiblenesse of that transmigration, I shall have
a joy, which shall no more evaporate, then my soule
shall evaporate, A joy, that shall passe up, and put on
a more glorious garment above, and be joy super-
invested in glory. *Amen.*

CAMBRIDGE
PLAIN TEXTS

The following Volumes are the latest
additions to this Series:

English

LANCELOT ANDREWES. Two Sermons.
With a Note by J. Butt and G. Tillotson.

JONSON. The Sad Shepherd.
With a Note by L. J. Potts.

GOWER. Selections from *Confessio Amantis*.
With a Note by H. S. Bennett.

French

MOLIÈRE. La Critique de l'École des Femmes
and L'Impromptu de Versailles.
With a Note by A. Tilley.

RONSARD. L'Art Poétique *and* Cinq Préfaces.
With a Note by J. Stewart.

German

HOFFMANN. Der Kampf der Sänger.
With a Note by G. Waterhouse.

LESSING. Hamburgische Dramaturgie I.
LESSING. Hamburgische Dramaturgie II.
With a Note by G. Waterhouse.

Spanish

OLD SPANISH BALLADS.
With a Note by J. P. Howard.

VILLENA: LEBRIJA: ENCINA. Selections.
With a Note by I. Bullock.

small octavo pages of text, preceded

note on the author

LIMP CLOTH

German

GRILLPARZER. Der Arme Spielmann *and* Erinnerungen an Beethoven.
HERDER. Kleinere Aufsätze I.
HOFFMANN. Der Kampf der Sänger.
LESSING. Hamburgische Dramaturgie I.
LESSING. Hamburgische Dramaturgie II.

Italian

ALFIERI. La Virtù Sconosciuta.
GOZZI, GASPARO. La Gazzetta Veneta.
LEOPARDI. Pensieri.
MAZZINI. Fede e Avvenire.
ROSMINI. Cinque Piaghe.

Spanish

BOLÍVAR, SIMÓN. Address to the Venezuelan Congress at Angostura, February 15, 1819.
CALDERÓN. La Cena de Baltasar.
CERVANTES. Prologues and Epilogue.
CERVANTES. Rinconete y Cortadillo.
ESPRONCEDA. El Estudiante de Salamanca.
LOPE DE VEGA. El Mejor Alcalde, el Rey.
LUIS DE LEÓN. Poesías Originales.
OLD SPANISH BALLADS.
VILLEGAS. El Abencerraje.
VILLENA: LEBRIJA: ENCINA. Selections.

SOME PRESS OPINIONS

www.ingramcontent.com/pod-product-compliance
Ingram Content Group UK Ltd.
Pitfield, Milton Keynes, MK11 3LW, UK
UKHW042148280225
455719UK00001B/191